Love between Sandwiches 2

Love between Sandwiches 2

Roger Pope

Roger H. Pope

Trimingham Press

First published in 2006 by Trimingham Press
39 Paddocks Lane, Cheltenham, Glos GL50 4NU
Email: rogerhughpope@aol.com

A catalogue record for this book is available from the British Library.

ISBN: 0 9529202 4 7 (978 0 9529202 4 3)

Designed and typeset by Authority Publishing
Set in Palatino

Printed in the UK by TJ International Ltd

To my wife, Jean

with many thanks for being the first audience
for every poem in my collection

– and to our children, Emma and Daniel

Some of these poems have appeared in:
Poetry Now,
Envoi,
The Frogmore Papers,
Folio and
Cotswold Life,
to whose editors thanks are due.

Contents

Love between Sandwiches 2

Love between Sandwiches

I opened
my see-through lunch box
and found
your folded note
hidden
between my sandwiches.

Then
I wished you here,
beside me,
sharing my lunch-life
with the lid off –
just two spring onions
intertwined
beneath a duvet of bread,
making love
on a bed of lettuce.

Between Friends

When, in the early hours,
I cannot sleep and come downstairs
To make a drink and read,
Or scribble a word or two;

When I light the fire
And watch the flames of gas
Come flickering across the coals,
Then it is that you come in from kitchen sleep,
Cat-silent, across the lounge.

The flames welcome your familiar face
And dance to your gazing eyes,
While the sensuous heat embraces
Your handsome chest and snow-white legs.

And when you are 'done',
You move to cleaning mode,
Following your feline routine with meticulous care;
After which, you lie down by the hearth,
Stretch out, relax and rest your eyes.

No word is ever passed between us,
Yet I welcome your company at such hours,
And you, I do believe, you welcome the fire.

Carried Away

'A fiver for the table,
but nothing for that.
Nobody wants 'em
these days – sideboards.'

For a moment, we stare
at our old family furniture.

His van is parked outside,
like a hearse –
functional, tactful –
awaiting the no-longer useful
items of life.

I laugh, awkwardly.

Is it disappointment I try to disguise?
Or the betrayal of old friends?

We manoeuvre the table
out of the house
and into the dealer's van.
The seven-foot sideboard follows,
like a coffin borne away.

The dealer smiles,
closes up the van.

'Nobody wants 'em, see.'

A crumpled note passes
from hand
        to hand
                to pocket.

May Hill
Gloucestershire

This they once called Yartleton Hill,
    From the Celtic, meaning 'round topped', still
A name that fits, that's suitable.
    Close to a thousand feet above sea-level,
An encampment of towering Scots pine
    Is assembled here, like a conquering clan
Claiming the hill. We gaze around
    The circling counties, admire the border ground,
The silvered Severn reflecting sunlight,
    The Forest, the Malverns, and Welsh hills receding.

The sky is blue-and-yellow bright,
    But crisp chilly March will keep us moving.
These are the early-in-the-year days we love
    When landscapes awaken with the life we crave.
A pine-cone is blown from its tree-top,
    Pin-balling off branches as it tumbles down –
The tall and the small of this Gloucestershire crown.

Bird of Prey

Blood-lusting bird flies low,
Cropping tops of horizontals
Bordering suburban boundaries,
In and out of tiny territories
In eye-blinks of time.

Assassin gate-crashes,
Scattering birds like grapeshot.
Eyes, hard as granite,
Home in on the collared-dove,
Home in on the chosen one.

Dove, in its contorted flight,
Flies against an upper window,
Falls to earth, concussed,
Its broad grey breast skyward,
Head limp, eyes closed.

Killer mounts the breast,
Talons secured like ice-picks.
Plucking away soft feathers,
Exposing warm breast,
Ripping flesh to redness,

Cannibalism begins . . .

A very grown-up Young Lady addresses her aged Bear

For those who once cared for a bear - or, perhaps, still do

I've decided I really must throw you out,
  'Cos you've been here far too long,
And you'll never be wanted by anyone else
  For it's me to whom you belong.

I'm sorry, but now I've no longer the room
  For a bear who is well past his best.
As I'm very grown-up, an adult, in fact,
  I don't need any threadbare guest.

If only I thought you might answer me back,
  I would know that I really can't grouse.
It would make me, at least, reconsider the case
  For not throwing you out of the house.

I wish you could be a more useful 'thing'
  That I'd need in a grown-up way?
At least there'd be reason to give you a home,
  More reason to let you stay.

Curse you for being so stupid and dumb,
  For being so useless a bear.
Don't think your brown eyes shining up at me now
  Will persuade me I ought to care.

What's that? Did you speak? Did you utter a sound?
  Is a tear running down your old cheek?
Oh, come and be cuddled at once, little friend;
  I love you, my precious antique.

Ritual of Fatherhood

There was something about 'first thing in the morning'
And listening to my father whistling and crooning,
Like Crosby, with bits of conversation
Passing between us during a rendition.

I'm looking in from our bathroom doorway,
Staring at his shaving-cream display,
Spellbound, as he raises his whiskered chin
To expose more throat and tauten his skin

In readiness for the eager razor's task.
'Do you want to watch?' he'd always ask
Before shaving upwards towards his jawbone,
Making comical sounds in his baritone

Voice, as the stubble and cream disappeared.
The narrow strip, through his morning beard,
Would remind me of a layering of early snow
We had swept away some time ago.

How many times, I wonder, had I stood
In awe of this ritual of fatherhood,
And a man's own space and way of behaving?
'Not too near, son – not while I'm shaving.'

Melodies would go on punctuating
The proceedings until my patient waiting
Would be rewarded and I could approach
The almost holy water and touch,

With finger-tip, the soft white lumps
Speckled thickly with the black stubble
Which had grown in the night, somehow like magic –
And quite beyond the grasp of a child's logic.

Kingswear Houses

As seen looking across from Dartmouth in Devon

I could almost
think them human,
the buildings
just across the river,
the houses built
– how long ago? –
to keep the Kingswear people
comfortable and snug.

The flat-faced houses
congregate like friends,
bumping shoulders,
cosseting each other,
tier on tier,
pastel-shaded
like sugar-coated almonds.

I see them
all facing in one direction,
as those standing seagulls do
in these Devon breezes.

I grasp my camera,
carefully focus,
frame this familiar view.
My button finger's ready.

Click!

Have I caught them all . . .
smiling?

Clearing Out

We cleared out your garage today,
Sorting out the rubbish first.
'But that's not rubbish!' I hear you say,
For you were never prepared to waste

What might prove useful. 'Could come in
Handy,' was the phrase. The obvious jumble
Went first, disposed of in the bin,
Or the boot of my car to go to that council

Place. It's easier now; endurable.
After you passed away, we spared
Ourselves the hurt . . . Later, it was possible
To cope with all our memories, to stare

At your bench, noticing signs of your past
Activity. You were there in spirit –
Almost. (But no, not quite.) You loved
To tinker with your car, put up the bonnet,

Audition the music of the engine, adjusting
Here and there to improve the legato
Phrasing, fine tune the tappets, listening
Carefully. It seems so long ago,

Yet often I wonder what you did
Last of all in here, what maintenance
Job you casually put aside,
Unfinished . . .

Flying to China

Today you fly to Beijing.
   I brainstorm 'China',
Come up with the *Tao te Ching*
   And Lao-Tzu. I remember

The Chinese meal in London,
   In Chinatown, and the novice attempt
With chopsticks. I can see Tiananman
   Square and the contempt

That student showed a certain tank.
   I think of Chinese takeaways,
Noodles and Chow Mein. I think
   Of beautiful Chinese art; I raise

My glass to anyone who can learn Chinese
   Or make head or tail of their intricate
Script of symbols. Please
   Don't persuade me to try it.

We look forward to hearing from you
   When you'll tell us about your real-time
Experience of China when you'll surely outdo
   My random list turned to rhyme.

Inheritance

At times,
I am you –
an echo,
reflection,
imitation.

Just a mannerism
gives the game away.

The inheritance
you left me
becomes more apparent
each day,

if only to me,
if only *in* me.

Window Woman

I gaze out from my patio window,
over the gravel
and slim Sweet William border.

I look across the lawn
to the sparrow-speckled bird-table
under the boughs
of the white-blossomed apple tree.

I glance to trellis fencing,
espalier fruit-trees, and then,
through the green gregarious leaves,
I see her there again,
at her bedroom window,
cloth in hand, circling, circling,
round and round her window panes.

Like a seductress of semaphore,
season by season, day by day,
she wipes away
whatever lingers too long
upon those soiled, spoiled window panes.
Oh, so attentive.

What primeval cleansing instinct
drives her to this silent litany
of window worship?
For she is, in truth,
a devoted window woman –
a lady of the habit.

* * *

Look! New white windows, uPVC,
were fitted there last week
and look a treat.
No condensation, no lingering mist,
no sins of omission
to spoil her view.

She looks out now, no cloth in hand,
to cleaner, clearer views,
then disappears from sight.

My eyes retreat to trellis fencing,
espalier fruit-trees,
sparrow sights, bird-table feuds,
to lawn and borders
neat and trim.

Yet still, just now and then,
I glance at her bedroom window
and wonder –
will she ever again,
with cloth in hand,
come to wipe the weather away?

Or is that sight of cleaning delight
now gone forever, forever . . . ?

Observing a Cruise Liner passing Malta, G.C.

She sails into my view and could well be
a silent movie legend from the past,
or some sea goddess from mythology.

Admire her shimmering whiteness, which is cast
against blue sea and sun-soaked Maltese sky –
a Mediterranean beauty unsurpassed.

The small-fry craft all seem to occupy
themselves like courtiers generally do, though more
like flotsam to this regal passer-by.

How easy to forget this island's war-
time past, the long ferocious battles fought
at sea and in the air and from ashore.

Against all odds, her courage held and brought
her victory – and the cross she never sought.

Blackthorn at Wainlode
by the Severn in Gloucestershire

Above this wintered wood,
High flying rackety rooks
Speckle a blue-white sky.

Below steep banks,
The blind and winding Severn
Threads through this Shire land,
Deaf to proud and distant bells
Pealing their Sunday best.

Whispers of a season's awakening
Are borne on a placid breeze.

Close by, thorns on twigs
Remind me of another day,
Another hill, and white petalled cups,
Too pure to touch,
Impart a peace more set apart
Than all our hallowed hopes.

Coming of Age

How, then, will it arrive, old age?
    Will it come with the clanging of bells,
Will headlines announce it on a front page,
    Like fireworks colouring a darkening sky?

Or like the first-fall of forecasted snow
    Settling unalarmingly down –
Something that even children know
    And welcome, though it brings the chill.

Will it arrive with the morning post?
    Or be discovered in a game of cards?
Will it greet us like a friendly host
    Who shakes our hand as a trusted friend?

Will someone someday boldly tell me:
    'This is your old age, day one',
Or will that day dawn and be
    Unnoticed, simply passing by?

Old age: the gleaning of the field of time,
    The wearying and wearing out of parts,
The grand finale of a kind of pantomime
    Of life we love and fear by turns.

Nostalgia

Before the car came,
       we walked and talked
       from here to there,
       hand in hand.

Before the car came,
       we packaged ourselves
       in green double-deckers,
       from town to country,
       two-to-the-hour,
       driver, conductor,
       upstairs for smoke,
       downstairs for air.

Before the car came,
       we courted beneath canopies
       of star-spotted skies,
       befriended the tide-turning moon
       whose brilliance bathed our kisses,
       or else, half-hidden and clouded,
       shrouded our night in mystery.

Before the car came,
       we knew the long roads home,
       would laugh under spring-sprinkled showers,
       escape to the out-of-town shelter
       where no-one ever waited – except us.
       And there we'd linger in the chilly dusk
       of an autumn evening
       or the warmth of a summer's night,
       and miss a bus or two.

But then, at last, came the car,
       and our love and our loving moved on.

Morte Point

Mortehoe, North Devon

We walk once more by bracken
And bright yellow coconut-smelling gorse,
Where sheep come cautiously close
And gulls glide overhead.

We search the busy blue waves
For that solitary seal we sometimes
Used to see and take delight in finding.
Rounding the grey-white point,

We pause and see ourselves
Soon paddling along the seashore
Of that distant sweeping bay,
Playing young lovers' games again.

We're holding hands once more
And laughter still dances between us,
Yet boats at sea seem, somehow, images
Of other boats from other days.

The Great Escape

Foreign tongues
Flutter in the summer air;
A flock of sound-bites
Chirrups like sparrows;
Sun-wrapped children
Explode in shrieks.
The great escape begins.

A European union
Of holidaymakers
Is pool-plotted and pampered
Beneath egg-yolk parasols
Poaching in the sun.

What stresses are left behind?
What traumas await the few,
Or preceded their flight to
This veneer of paradise freedom?

For another year, perhaps,
The magic has been worked,
The spoiling has been done.

Too soon, the packaged dream
To sunshine will be over;
Normality will resume
Its predictable term of office.

Minus One

Even this summer's day is cold.

Minus one.

I leave room for you
on your half of our bed.
Your pillow is soft and welcoming
but the sheet is cold.

Minus one.

My side of the bed is warm,
in the hope that one day ...
but, no, you never will.

How is it that minus one
can be so cold?
So cold, the heart freezes,
even on a summer's day.

Without you, everything is minus,

and one is so lonely.

Cider with Poesy

Yes, there's room in this world for us,
We folk who weave words
And scribble on scraps of paper in pubs.

Cider sets itself to work
And sentences seek me out
Like pangs of hunger
Searching for food.

I am the consummate consumer,
The optimist of cidermania,
The manager of words.
I am cider-wise.

This is the draft I anticipate,
Whetting my appetite for pub grub
And stanzas of *joie de vivre*.
New lines arrive, waiter-less
Though waited for.

The forbidden fruit was plucked,
Pressed and drunk,
And now I am cast out,
Adrift on a cider-sea
Of creativity.

This is the course I'm set upon,
This is the starter.

Come forth, main course!

I Cannot Swim

I cannot swim in the dark.
This dark is too dense,
Too busy with thoughts
That swim better than I,
That sink me down, and down . . .

I cannot swim in the dark.
This dark has faces
That look familiar –
Loss, guilt, regret;
They sink me down, and down . . .

I cannot swim in the dark.
My dark is primeval,
Like ice, fire, blood,
Like breath . . . like memory.
And drowning is forbidden.

Me, You, Us

ME:

> a loose end,
> a puzzle unsolved,
> a jungle of threads,
> a pattern undiscerned.

YOU:

> a perfect circle,
> a disc of golden warmth,
> a hole in the midnight sky,
> a roulette of winning numbers,
> a button to do myself up with,
> a ring at the end of a telephone.

US:

> at a loose end,
> running around in circles,
> playing games with words.

The Day

It ought to be just another day,
Like yesterday or the day before.

It ought to be just another day
Of grass growing, of birds feeding,
And the world busy with itself.

I could have woken out of sleep
And noticed the little muscle-aches
That grow with the days;
Or observed the sliver of sunlight
Cutting in between cotton curtains.

Then I'd yawn like a tired old dog.
I'd get up, ponder the day I'd woken to
And mingle it with cereal and milk.

Perhaps I did these things
But didn't notice the day starting.
Maybe it *is* just another day.

Maybe the difference is me
Being just half what I was
With you.

Reflection

They say
that men are more spatial,
women more verbal.

But she
fills my eyes
with beauty

and I
have only words
to tell her so.

Space Craft

Your space and mine
bump against each other,
now and then.

But when all is said and done,
our spaces travel lightly
and are comfortable together.

They overlap
like shadow upon shadow,
like hand in hand.

With nonchalant ease,
our spaces move
unwittingly,
like gentle breathing
in the early hours.

Requiescat in Pace

These are the flowers you'll never see;
These are the flowers to you, from me.

These are the blooms you'll never touch,
The colours you always admired so much.

Above is the blue and the white of the sky,
The sun that we welcomed, birds flying by.

Here is the grass beneath my feet,
That covers you now, trimmed and neat.

This is your home of peace and rest,
Your plot of earth, forever blessed.

And here are the words you will never read:
'My greatest love, my life, my need.'

Coupled in Heaven

We're suited to each other,
Made to measure,
A perfect coming together
Of eyes to eyes,
Nose to nose,
Lips to lips.

Your smile triggers my smile,
Your laughter
Trips after
Mine –
Cause and effect
Ad infinitum.

Our time has come
For surely the gods have sprung
This perfect surprise -
A midnight sunrise.

Imagine the countdown,
Imagine the lift-off
As we cast off
All limitations,
All inhibitions.

Suspended in space,
We'll dock together
And orbit our wacky world
Of ecstasy
In our blinding
Star Trek fantasy.

Lust ... Lost

They close in like birds of prey
Pouncing upon carrion –
So quick, their blood pulsing.

Their eyes wantonly wander,
Flitting and flirting eagerly,
Their lust lingering like heat.

They caress, collude, fuse
Like dancers bonding their bodies;
A union of flesh, a raw rhythm.

*   *   *

One couple, two cups of coffee,
Two tiny islands spinning
In opposite directions.

Bubbles ride on carousel surfaces
Of cup-deep oceans;
The silence of eyes, concealing.

Two people, a Siamese corpse
Of dead emotions;
Lovers, losers ... lost.

Inscribed: 'Bill – Colchester, January 1946'

This slender book seems like some bequest
  Left me by a man I never knew.
Or perhaps I play the part of the privileged guest
  Of a certain Bill, with this beguiling clue:

'Colchester, January 1946'.
  These poems that he would've read were clearly a gift
From a thoughtful friend, and though not war-time classics
  Like others that come to mind, I like the drift

Of what the poet had wanted to say. I find
  Myself drawn back to them, time after time,
Re-reading poems that have lingered in my mind,
  Enjoying a line, a phrase, a particular rhyme.

Bill will never know by whom his book
  Was bought. As second-hand and rather plain,
It could have been so easy to overlook
  The fading spine, the name: John Jarmain.

Nothing To Say

There is nothing to say
    That tomorrow will be there
Till you wake and find
    The world unwrapped and ready.

There is nothing to say
    That all the planets and stars
Will impress or concern you more
    Than the slow drip of your leaking tap.

And I can tell you, too,
    That every breath you take
Will question the time you spend
    Mundanely rethinking the past.

You will discern for yourself
    The countenance upon the world's face
As you set foot upon tomorrow
    And scuttle through your day.

And at the end of it all,
    Words will have been mere shadows,
For the substance of life is love discovered
    In your brief safari of chance.

Jungle

I lift up the young starling
From a huddle of fallen leaves,
Caging it securely in my interlocking
Hands. Between my fingers and thumbs,
A narrow skull and streamlined beak
Thrust up and swivel like a turret-gun.

Cat's eyes, secreted in foliage,
Lock on like laser beams.
The cat crouches, seeking advantage,
Tense, drunk with adrenalin, motionless.
This tiger of the garden schemes
Cleverly and waits to be ruthless.

Modigliani 1884-1920

Take a straight line
and give it to Amedeo
who will journey with it
where he will.

He will show you
the line of simplicity.

He will curve the line just so,
here, and here;
the curves will be more, or less.

The woman will be reclining,
naked and at ease –
elegant, erotic, tender.

And when the gentle line
has run its sinuous course,
and its subtle rhythm has ceased,
the straight line will be
but a memory, transformed,
transcended.

Sunrise 2000

Observed in Gloucestershire on January 1st 2000

Grey early morning,
Tired eyes struggle open,
Intentions wriggle uncomfortably.
Inner conflicts reach 'deuce',
Move to 'advantage sunrise'
And then . . .

Expeditious exit to outside.
Nostrils vacuum up fresh air;
Birds are singing like chirrupy children;
Houses give way to hilltop silhouettes;
Skyline brightens slowly to fireglow.

Watch: don't miss the top of the sun.
Don't look around, not now.
Counting down . . .

Then, swift as a blink,
Brilliance bursts upwards,
Silent explosion of sunlight,
Instant switch-on of cosmic floodlights.
Eyes constantly scan left and right,
Snatching at the sunrise.

The shimmering arc expands,
Awesome sunpower,
Reaches diameter point;
Slowly, slowly, floats clear:
Sunbirth from the hills.

Starship 2000
Ascends into heaven.

Rabbit on the Beach

Half-blind, ugly-eyed,
Myxomatosis afflicted,
The rabbit lollops along the beach,
Pauses, as if to ponder,
Goes slowly on towards the tide.

Children are compassionate
But do not touch.
They stay close by,
Crouching down,
Eyeing intently.

Rabbit meanders away
Through the shallow water,
Alone, isolated, incongruous.

Left behind are the uncomfortable
And curious people who watch
And follow with puzzled eyes.

Like a strange dream,
It seems there should be meaning here;
But it is as it is –
No meaning, no symbol, no hope.

Jam-jar Blues

Marmalade is kept in jars;
That's the way it has to be,
For marmalade is rather loose
And needs to be contained, you see?

Now she was marmalade, so golden;
He was jam-jar, clear and plain.
She was known for what she was,
And that was 'tricky to contain'.

For she, by nature, sweet as jam,
Was too inclined to spread herself
On tanned and toasted tasty youths
Who loved a breakfast off the shelf.

Soon marmalade was out and gone,
Elsewhere and everywhere adored.
She left him with those jam-jar blues,
Quite alone, depressed and bored.

No fun to be an empty jar
When jammy worlds just fall apart.
No doubt a dustbin graveyard loomed –
A rubbish end to break his heart.

But then, ye fruity gods, oh then
A luscious strawberry sidled by,
As sexy as a fruit can be
With friends who really were not shy.

She fired his heart with tempting talk
Of how she longed for life inside,
Then she and friends just filled right in
His jam-jar space – he felt such pride.

And so he gently closed his lid,
Contained her as his type will do.
They both confessed that this was love –
Jam-packed passion, through and through.

At last he felt a proper jar,
Joy unbounded, you'll agree.
His fruitful love was now contained,
Content to be preserved, you see?

Corner-cutting

If you corner-cut through from the High Street,
Cast a glance at the smart old bowling green

With its proud white-painted club house
And battalion of immaculate black railings.

You'll not avoid the recently opened phone shop
Catering for all needs in mobile conversation.

But then pause in the derelict graveyard
By the old and newly converted chapel,

Converted to commerce, we hear,
By more persuasive profits.

Headstones lie like Custer's soldiers:
Broken, dead and largely forgotten.

Nettles hang about like ragged mourners;
Incongruous saplings survive by neglect.

Perhaps you'll pass swiftly over these lost lives
Whose eternities seem to rest in chiselled words,

Their passing through this world as brief
And inconsequential as anyone's corner-cutting.

The Beach

The metal detector swings
From side to side
In its simple silent rhythm,
Sweeping the beach
Like a giant coin searching
For lost relatives,
Ignoring home-going families
With their sun-burnt bodies
And their chided children.

Snow-feathered gleaners
Glide, flap, scoop,
Hover, and fall,
Touch down briefly,
Rise with captured crusts.
Would-be thieves give chase,
Give up, squall their protest.

The sea ebbs and flows,
Indifferent to left-behind litter
Which, by stealth,
It swallows, gulp by gulp,
Licking the beach clean
For tomorrow's people.

The rusty old sea-dog tractors
Wait patiently on the beach –
Their boats are coming home.

We Pretend

Only you and me for this reunion.
Now the seats sag a little and the music,
No longer laid back, intrudes
When once it harmonised our mood.

No familiar faces here, none
To stir our memories; so we succumb
To predictable reminiscing, run
In vain through names with the barman.

We study the menu, noting trendy
Changes, smile approvingly, but suspend
Our hunger a little longer. We pretend
That nothing's changed, that nothing ended.

A View of Heaven

Sunday morning. I draw back
The bedroom curtains and ease back into bed,
Duvet-covered in comfort and mind-mocking
The clock's irrelevance. Scrunching up
My weak unspectacled eyes towards the window,
I see surrealist Dali doves in white window catches.

The glazed canvas conveys a brilliant
Sky-washed blue, the blue that only sky creates,
Sky illumined now by off-stage sun.

A few white islands, ethereal, soft,
Bathe lazily in a sea of Caribbean sky.
A flock of flying specks drifts slowly across.

Spectacled now, the familiar view sharpens,
Eyesight flattered by heightened autumn light.

Three funnels on a roof-top boat appear;
Crowns of trees infill spaces with gold,
Conifer green, yellows and dappled bronze.

Aerials perch on ends of houses
Like Picasso-sculpted storks.
Under the eaves outside,
The reddened Boston ivy clings tenaciously.

Sky reasserts its presence, moulds my mood,
Saturates my senses, stirs my mind to create.
For certain I know that words will come, surely
If only to share some view, this view, of heaven.

Inside Love

I want to wheedle my way into your sadness
And find a corner of your mind
Where you and I can touch.

Please don't shut me out but leave me access
To your loneliness; be kind
To one who loves you so much.

Place of No Return

I've decided I'll *not*
   Come here again,
Not in the sunshine,
   Nor in the rain,
For it seems to have caused
   A return of the pain.

Yet I'd like to have thought
   I could cope with the strain
Of coming back here
   With you on my brain.
But no, I'm afraid
   It's so dreadfully plain:

Memories hurt
   When the dragon's not slain.

Picasso at the Tate 1994

I try to de-cube, rearrange his puzzle,
Find an eye, a breast, a leg.
My spectacles help me see
But not with Pablo's eyes.
A genius with odds and ends, I'm told.

In terms of Art, I guess I'm just a peasant
Who needs an eye to be an eye,
A breast a breast, a leg a leg, et cetera –
More or less. But as it is, I notice

Too much breast, too little or none at all.
The urge to cut along the lines,
Move the shapes around
Becomes a curious urge.
Would it work? I imagine it, doubt it.

The Mellow Years

When the busy years give way to rest,
When memories gather, contenting themselves
With second-best;

When long-forgotten plans and schemes
That mattered so much have had their day,
No longer dreams;

Will the shadow cast by common fears
Unsettle the easy peace and poise
Of our mellow years?

Or will that gleam of love in our eyes
Help ease the thoughts which time refuses
To disguise?

Invigilation

School ties, symbols of solidarity,
Hang limp between rolled-up sleeves.
Heads, held angle-poised like reading lamps,
Survey the word-littered landscapes.
Anxious fingers fidget with pens
While prostrate virgin sheets await attack.

A summer sniff snuffles around the room
Shadowed by vagrant flies seeking an open window.
Ancient idle gods are here,
Sitting aloof on table-tops.
Time passes, quartz-crystal silent.
Time, tickless time passes ...

'English Literature – Unseen Appreciation'.
So what will they make of you now, Heaney?
What will they make of you – NOW?

Taking Leave

At times, she really makes no sense
At all. She simply seems to ramble
On and on, appearing tense,
Afraid, her thoughts and speech a jumble.

This really cannot be my mother,
Widowed wife, loved so long
By him whom she forgets. Another
Day when everything seems wrong.

She asks me: 'Am I going mad?'
We avoid the word 'dementia'. I grieve
For who she was, what's lost. So sad
That this is how she'll take her leave.

I sense she knows I understand
Just what it is she fears to name.
She's comforted when I hold her hand
And say those things, always the same,

Which seem to give her just some slight
Relief. And yet I know that I
Must now accept that this is twilight
Time for her, a darkening of her sky.

Staying at the Manor

'We'd like *en suite* facilities, colour TV,
A south facing room with a view of the sea;
Bed, breakfast and evening meal.
Your five-day break seems an excellent deal.

Just one room left, then the hotel's full?
Of course, half-term – they're all off school.
The room you've just mentioned – a double bed?
A double's preferred. Oh, it's twin beds instead.'

A shame, not a double, we hear ourselves think.
Never mind, we accept – with a nod and a wink.
We sign ourselves in, give our car registration,
Complete all essential administration.

Then it's up to our room on the second floor,
With all regulations pinned up on the door.
We unpack our cases, put all things away,
Then study the tips for an enjoyable stay.

The room's very clean, the décor is fine.
We're hungry and thirsty and eager to dine.
We shower and dress and hope for the best,
Optimistic and ready for well-earned rest.

Descending the stairs, we aim for the bar
Which beckons us in. We won't need a car
With no driving to do. Thank goodness for that.
We can eat, drink, mingle and chat.

With our thirst now quenched, the menu at last.
Four courses for dinner, the choice is vast.
The waitress arrives with her notepad and pen,
Writes down our choices of dishes, and then

'A bottle of Merlot would be very nice',
I request (we had noted the reasonable price).
The starters prove splendid, the main courses great.
Desserts? Fantastic and well worth the wait.

Coffee to finish, with whisky and cream.
They call it a Gaelic; I called it a dream.
Our stomachs are bursting, my trousers are tight,
Caused by this huge gastronomic delight.

We make it upstairs, feeling tipsy and fat,
Undress – just about – but too tired to chat.
Two people collapse into two welcome beds.
The room's spinning round. Is it just in our heads?

Fingertips touch over space in between,
With giggles completing the comical scene.
Stupor sets in and limbs are like lead.
Then a snuffled 'Goodnight!' from each little twin bed.

Red Square, Moscow 1995

The souls of my shoes
    insulate the reality
    of being here:
    Red Square,
    awesome solid history.

And so,
    like a laughing child,
    I crouch down and press
    my outstretched hands
    upon the cobbled blue-grey bricks.

A startling thought:
    Kruschev might've done this,
    Kennedy couldn't –
    I have.

And Lenin in his mausoleum:
    we file past in half-light, half-dark,
    a caterpillar of apprehension
    moving slowly, solemnly.
    Silent queue, shuffled thoughts.

Untouchable revolutionary,
    entombed in glass,
    as neat as a wax work,
    silenced and death-blind.
    Will the armed guards blink?

The high-walled glorious Kremlin,
    world of secrets and splendour,
    plaques galore along this lofty wall.
    Interred just here is Yuri Gagarin.
    I remember his newspaper face
    beaming around the world.

But who was this Arthur McMannus?

The Old Drop-out

He has been forgotten,
That old man sitting in the square,
Scratching his defunct face
Beneath grey and greasy hair.

He travels alone,
Overcoated and tied
With string – a parcel big enough
To shrink into and hide.

He sleeps in a box,
Or on a bench. They say
He just drifted from family and friends,
Gave up and lost his way.

He is falling to bits,
Like an overcooked rabbit;
But he owns his bones and skin.
Ignoring him is merely habit.

Collectable

I find you
Squeezed in upon the shelf,
Half-hidden from the public gaze.

A slim and alluring shyness,
A certain mystery, intrigues me.
I am tempted,
I pause . . .

Then, running my finger down your spine,
I remove you from your shelf.
For the moment, I possess you,
Bare your words to my eyes,
Exposing your chosen charms.

Your subtle words awaken my senses;
Your opening gambit has me reeling.
I am lost, vanquished.

Whispering your discovered name,
I consider the cost . . .
Together, we elope.

Finding you

I love to find you in the night-time,
When your toes rest, child-like, upon my legs;
To be stirred by the warmth of your body –
Naked, smooth, slow-breathing, sleeping . . .
The smell of your hair, your pillowed head
Sheltering under my arm.
So we cheat the waking, working hours.

The green-glow figures of time
Play gooseberry in the dark,
Unmasking each newborn minute
In the silence of bird-sleeping hours.

Time will not stand still for us
Nor life be more than earth;
Yet more ancient hearts than ours knew,
Like us, the intimate quiet of night.

Feather-wise

The swallows left early this year,
Which means an early winter,
They say, and a bitter one at that.
Strange how swallows know such things
And leave much sooner than expected.
There are other birds, of course,
That stay through frost and snow.
Sometimes there is fear of going,
But survival is the heart of it all.

And so she went, enduring frost-bite
Of the senses, fearing an arctic death.
Spring had been good, summer as perfect
As a skylark's song. But autumn was
Strangely languid, and on the borders
Of winter, panic set in, like an antelope
Twitching its nose, stalked by its fate,
Uncertain of danger's whereabouts.
'Making it through', she'd said, 'is survival,
And, yes, finding the sun in winter.'

Vacant Possession

The street has never been neighbourly.
Houses are scarred with neglect,
Windows droop with melancholy
And doors are securely locked.

Her face appears quite often,
Like a snowdrop in scrubby earth.
She observes from behind net curtains
Which reveal her but veil the truth.

The walls are so stiff upper-lipped
And always beyond noticing things.
In evenings, under lampshaded light,
She craves for warmth – and wings.

Russian Snapshot 1995

Along the rough and potholed roads, clustered
In patient idleness with dull faces wrinkled
Like old peaches too long in the sun,
The women, in weather-faded headscarves, shun
All eye contact, look blankly elsewhere.
Their produce (vegetables, fruit) is set out with care
On boxes and small tables. No smiling talk
Or chatter; only seeming indifference. I walk
By, uncomfortably tarnished by trappings of affluence.

My zoom-lens camera hangs awkwardly, its evidence
Stored like dark secrets, to be passed in a whisper.
Across a gourmet table, I'll talk of Russia:
'Photos can't reveal it all', I'll say,
'Poverty, apathy, shortage, neglect.' I'll convey
It as best as I can. And yet they'll understand
Familiar things – like the multi-grand
Russian BMWs, series seven,
Owned by entrepreneurs, buying and selling.

Back View

She arranges the flowers,
Rearranges them,
Nervously touches a bloom.

They are like obedient children,
Tidy and admired.

She removes the framed photos,
Dusts them, replaces them,
Finely judges their spacing.

He watches from his armchair,
Uncomfortably aware of memory
Twitching in her mind.
She pauses . . .

His eyes are obedient children
Who watch, think, say nothing.

Just now, he is glad of her back,
Avoiding her anxious eyes.

Modern Man

You live a takeaway life,
Discarding your throwaway days
Like empty cartons.

You skim over days
Like the pages of yesterday's newspaper.
Your blank early-bird brain
Awakes each morning
To the impress of another day.

How proud you are,
Living in the 'real world'
Where everything counts –
And nothing matters.

Beyond your 'real world',
You see drop-outs and burnt-outs,
Hedgerow Henrys and lean green guys.
'Getting on' is your game
And you made it by forty –
Status and a golden ulcer.

But today you are Mr Nobody.
Rationalised to expendability,
You backtrack a mile or two,
Searching for those footpaths
You neglected on your way.

How It Is

Waiting . . .
For beginnings, endings,
For things to happen,
Things to change;
Like a chameleon accustomed
To colour-scheming.

Things *will* change.
In any event, you must keep moving.
So I wait as I move, and move as I wait.
There's the nonsense.

Waiting . . .
Let's jump and fall for a month or two,
Until . . . Not coming?
Then I'll jump alone
And meet you, sometime.

Where? you ask.
In the mist of mystery,
Or perhaps the mist of mistake.

Waiting is not a game, not a vacation.
It's how it is – all the time.

Time . . . to wait around, see what happens;
Guess the moment the balloon will burst
And blast your face away with the emptiness
That was inside . . . all the time.

The Planets
– or, at least, two of them

There are you on *your* planet
And here am I on *mine*,
Thus the gravity of loving
Keeps apart what should combine.

The stars around shine brightly on,
The sky seems full of promise,
But your planet's looking rather rough,
Your weather full of malice.

Now look at me, my planet's fine,
It's spinning like a top.
Its hue is quite remarkable;
I wouldn't care to swop.

What's that you say, it's just conceit,
My ego's far too male?
It's *me* that's in a mood? Come on,
The truth's another tale.

Okay, we must avoid a crash,
I'm hearing what you say.
Our planets are quite different, yes,
With that I'm quite *au fait*.

Your planet's just a little tired,
That's why it's got a wobble?
All right, I'll try to understand
And not cause all this trouble.

I'm sorry if our planets are
Not always quite in tune.
Perhaps in future orbits
We can both spin round the moon.

Your weather's clearing up, I see,
It's turning brilliant blue.
I can feel the pull of gravity,
At last it's proving true.

Look out! We're closing far too fast,
A dangerous rendezvous.
If only we had lived upon
One planet less than two.

Our true love's course was never smooth –
Oh, let it all go hang.
We might as well go out in style
With one great cosmic bang!

For Shirley 'Someone'

These flowers, wrapped as a gift
And left beneath this tree
On the verge by this busy road,
Seem lost, floating adrift
Like a wreath upon the sea –
A tragic episode.

I crouch down low to read:
'For Shirley, R. I. P.'
Then a day, a month, a year.
In time, does grief recede?
The flowers will die but she
Is being remembered here

By those whose love she knew.
Few words; what little is said
Befits a benediction.
I wonder, Shirley, just who
You were, what life you'd led,
What laughter's now been stolen.

Full Circle

Our childless time is a dimming-down memory
Of our coupled life, now framed in photos.

Years have passed with the swiftness
Of a long sleeping and a sudden awakening.

Now our fledglings have left
And we cannot turn time back again.

So where will life take us,
Now they both have flown?

What shall we find there or rediscover?
Will it bruise us or treat us kindly?

For sure, we'll often look out of windows
To watch them moving on . . .

Childless for a while.

Birth of a Poem

Words trickle from my fingers
Like raindrops down window panes.
The pen transmutes my thoughts
To clustered symbols, to ordered chains
Of words. So language shapes
Images conceived inside my mind
And moulds the meaning thought began.
Each drafted phrase is honed, refined,
Auditioned by the inner ear and voice
And so within its space confined.

The poem is born, imperfectly composed,
Coupled to the page, vulnerable, exposed.